J   4374807
567.9   17.27
Ame
Amery
Looking at--Brachiosaurus

DATE DUE			

SK

GREAT RIVER REGIONAL LIBRARY

St. Cloud, Minnesota 56301

GAYLORD MG

Looking at . . . Brachiosaurus
A Dinosaur from the JURASSIC Period

THE NEW
Dinosaur
COLLECTION

4374807

For a free color catalog describing Gareth Stevens's list of high-quality books, call 1-800-341-3569 (USA) or 1-800-461-9120 (Canada).

Library of Congress Cataloging-in-Publication Data

Amery, Heather.
    Looking at-- Brachiosaurus/written by Heather Amery; illustrated by Tony Gibbons.
       p. cm. -- (The New dinosaur collection)
    Includes index.
    Summary: Describes the physical characteristics and probable behavior of this long-necked dinosaur.
    ISBN 0-8368-1044-9
    1. Brachiosaurus--Juvenile literature. [1. Brachiosaurus. 2. Dinosaurs.] I. Gibbons, Tony, ill.
II. Title. III. Series.
QE862.S3A437 1993
567.9'7--dc20   93-25687

This North American edition first published in 1993 by
Gareth Stevens Publishing
1555 North RiverCenter Drive, Suite 201
Milwaukee, Wisconsin 53212 USA

This U.S. edition © 1993 by Gareth Stevens, Inc. Created with original
© 1993 by Quartz Editorial Services, Premier House, 112 Station Road,
Edgware HA8 7AQ U.K.

Consultant: Dr. David Norman, Director of the Sedgwick Museum of Geology,
University of Cambridge, England.

All rights reserved. No part of this book may be reproduced, stored in a
retrieval system, or transmitted in any form or by any means, electronic,
mechanical, photocopying, or otherwise, without the prior written
permission of the copyright holder.

Printed in MEXICO
2 3 4 5 6 7 8 9 98 97 96 95 94 93

At this time, Gareth Stevens, Inc., does not use 100 percent recycled paper, although the paper
used in our books does contain about 30 percent recycled fiber. This decision was made after a
careful study of current recycling procedures revealed their dubious environmental benefits.
We will continue to explore recycling options.

Looking at . . . Brachiosaurus
A Dinosaur from the JURASSIC Period

by Heather Amery

Illustrated by Tony Gibbons

THE NEW
DINOSAUR
COLLECTION

Gareth Stevens Publishing
MILWAUKEE

Contents

Introducing
Brachiosaurus

Brachiosaurus (BRACK-EE-OH-SAW-RUS) was a giant. It was one of the biggest and heaviest dinosaurs that ever lived. It was also one of the tallest, with an enormously long neck to reach right up to the treetops. A giraffe – if it had existed in Jurassic times – would only have reached up to its shoulders. And, even if you stretched, you would hardly have been able to touch its knees.

It lived about 145 million years ago.

Its bones have been found in those parts of the world that are now the United States and parts of Africa.

Brachiosaurus means "arm lizard." It was given this name because its front legs, unlike those of most dinosaurs, were longer than its back ones. In many ways, both the front and back legs were like pillars, supporting its tremendous body weight.

How much do scientists know about **Brachiosaurus**? Turn the following pages to find out all about this long-necked dinosaur.

Towering monster

Brachiosaurus's neck was so long that, if it were not extinct, it could look over the roof of a three-story house. From its snout to the end of its powerful tail, it was as long as a tennis court. And it weighed as much as several fully grown elephants.

It had massive, stumpy legs to carry its body weight of up to 70 tons, and short, thick toes. Underneath each foot was a thick pad that protected its bones from jarring on the ground as it walked.

Because it was so big, **Brachiosaurus** could not move as quickly as some smaller dinosaurs. But it had a long stride and covered huge distances fairly quickly. If you had been able to stand next to a **Brachiosaurus**, it would have towered high above you.

Brachiosaurus would sway its neck and turn its head from side to side when feeding. It must also have had a very large and powerful heart to pump blood all the way up its long neck to its brain.

Some scientists suggest it may have had a specially designed heart to help circulate its blood all around its enormous body. Others think it may even have had two hearts to help with this work.

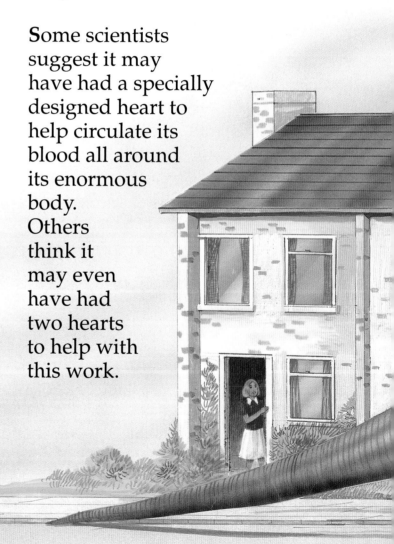

Although **Brachiosaurus** was big, its head was small and broad, and it had a very small brain for the size of its body. Its nostrils were very large and on top of its head.

Brachiosaurus's neck operated very much like a crane does today and was moved by a system of ribs and powerful muscles. The bones in its neck were lightweight, so it could raise and lower the neck quite easily.

At first, it was thought that **Brachiosaurus** might have had a trunk like the elephants we know today. But scientists no longer think so.

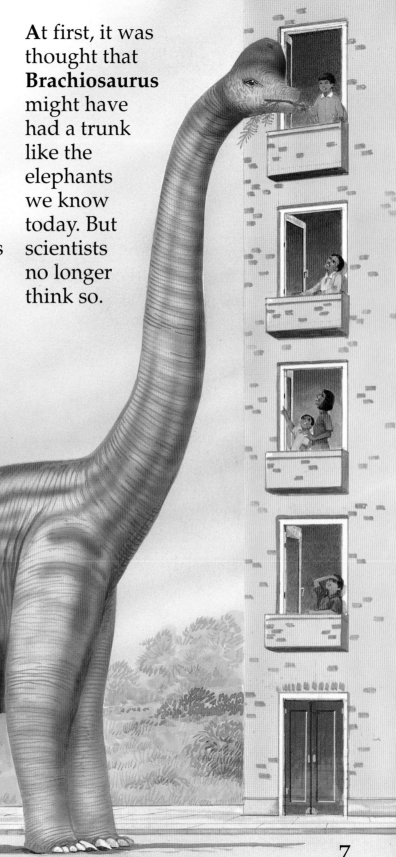

7

Long-necked skeleton

Brachiosaurus had a very strong framework of bones to hold up its enormous body. The most noticeable thing about its skeleton was its long neck.

Balancing this great neck was a long tail. **Brachiosaurus** could swing its tail from side to side and probably raised it off the ground when walking.

Its legs were very powerful and thick, like an elephant's. The front legs were longer than the back ones. Each of its broad feet had five short toes.

Brachiosaurus ate so much it had a huge stomach.

It, therefore, needed to support all this weight on four sturdy legs. **Brachiosaurus** probably could not rear up on its back legs like some dinosaurs. But its neck was so long it would not have needed to do this anyway.

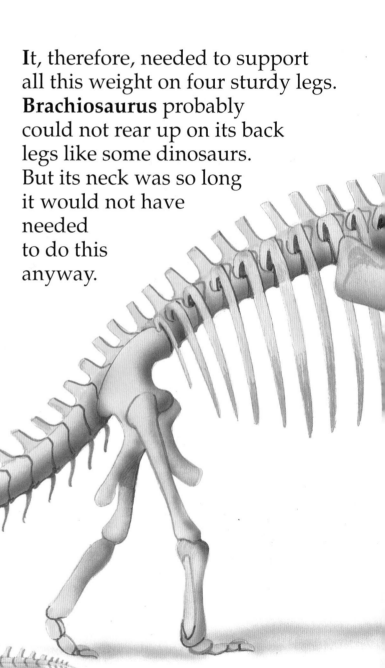

Notice how its massive backbone was arched to hold the weight of its enormous body.

Brachiosaurus was so strong it might even have been able to carry almost half its own weight – perhaps as much as 30 tons – on its back.

Scientists once thought that **Brachiosaurus** lived in lakes and rivers. They imagined that the water would have helped hold up its huge body and that it could have fed on soft water plants.

Brachiosaurus must have held its legs very straight as it walked. It was so heavy that, if it had bent its legs too much, the bones might have broken under all that weight.

Attached to the backbone were long rib bones to protect its lungs and stomach.

Muscles that stretched from its back and up its neck were useful in helping **Brachiosaurus** hold up its head without too much effort.

Now, however, scientists believe **Brachiosaurus** lived for most of the time on land, only occasionally paddling in water. If it had lived in water, its ribs might have been crushed by the weight of the water, and it would not have been able to breathe easily.

Notice how small the skull seems when you compare it with the rest of **Brachiosaurus's** body. But it was actually longer than your arm.

9

African discovery

One of the biggest and most complete dinosaur skeletons ever found was of a **Brachiosaurus**.

A German scientist hunting for minerals in Tanzania, Africa, about 85 years ago came across some huge bones at a place called Tendaguru.

He reported his remarkable find, and a dig was soon organized.

The African dig lasted four years. There was a lot of hard work to be done.

All the bones found had to be carried to the nearest port over 40 miles (65 km) away.
The people helping on the dig made over 5,000 trips to the port and carried 250 tons of dinosaur bones.

Among all the bones shipped out of Africa were those of a **Brachiosaurus**. The gigantic rebuilt skeleton is now on display in a museum in Berlin, Germany, where it has a place of honor.

It has been described as the most impressive dinosaur skeleton in the world, standing 39 feet (12 m) tall and 74 feet (23 m) long.

11

Jurassic life

Herds of **Brachiosaurus** roamed plains and forests in the Jurassic Period about 160–145 million years ago. Feeding on the tallest trees, they trampled great paths through the ferns that grew thickly on the ground. They left trails of footprints and droppings.

At that time, the climate was warm and damp.

The first birds flew overhead, and huge pterosaurs flapped through the air on leathery wings.

Herds of **Brachiosaurus** were always on the lookout for meat-eating dinosaurs.

13

Massive meals

Brachiosaurus ate only plants. With its long neck, it could feed on the tallest trees, picking off leaves and twigs for its meals. The trees were too high for other plant-eating dinosaurs to reach.

Some scientists think **Brachiosaurus** also ate water plants, stretching its neck down to feed from the banks of rivers or lakes.

It must have eaten a huge amount of food to make enough energy to power its massive body. An elephant eats about 330 pounds (150 kg) of food a day. **Brachiosaurus**, ten times bigger, needed a great deal more.

Because of the tremendous amount of leaves and plants that **Brachiosaurus** ate every day, scientists think its droppings must have been the most enormous heaps!

After **Brachiosaurus** had gulped down its food, special muscles pounded the plants to a mush between rough pebbles that the dinosaur had swallowed for this purpose.

Life in the herd

Brachiosaurus probably lived in family groups or small herds of up to 20 dinosaurs.

Because the fully grown adults were so large and needed so much food, the herd may have moved on to find new grazing grounds each day.

When they had stripped all the leaves off the tops of one clump of trees, they wandered on to the next clump and fed there, too. They did not bother about leaves farther down the tree. It would have been a strain on their necks, so lower leaves were left for smaller dinosaurs to eat.

As the herds traveled, the young dinosaurs were watched and guarded by the large adults that left the huge, deep footprints that still exist in the soft ground.

When threatened by a big meat-eating dinosaur hunting for a meal, the young would run to their mothers for safety. The big males may then have surrounded the rest of the herd to protect them from a predatory carnivore.

A newly hatched **Brachiosaurus** was probably quite small. Scientists think it had a soft skin at first that became tough and scaly as it grew older.

It may have taken many years before a **Brachiosaurus** grew into a full-sized adult and was ready to mate and have its own young.

The sight of a large herd of these huge Jurassic creatures must have been amazing.

17

Protecting the family

A family of **Brachiosaurus** fed quietly on a clump of trees. When they had eaten all the best leaves, they would then move on, trudging through the thick ferns.

Suddenly, an **Allosaurus** (<u>AL</u>-OH-<u>SAW</u>-RUS) ran out of the trees.

The small dinosaurs stayed close to their mothers, where it was safest. Meanwhile, the big males lumbered along beside them.

It chased a young **Brachiosaurus**. The **Allosaurus** was hungry. Its great jaws gaped open, showing long, sharp teeth.

18

It had not dared attack an adult **Brachiosaurus**. Instead, it had gone straight for a young one, sinking its teeth into the soft neck.

The **Allosaurus** staggered, dropped the baby, and tried to bite the big tail as it struck again. The baby squealed before it died. **Brachiosaurus** had lost its young. It managed to rear up on its back legs and crashed its front legs down on **Allosaurus's** head. The attacker fell to the ground, its skull crushed and its back broken. It, too, was now dead.

A big male **Brachiosaurus** turned and charged the **Allosaurus** as it dragged the baby away, striking the predator with its tail.

Brachiosaurus data

Brachiosaurus, with its long neck and massive body, was one of the largest dinosaurs ever to have walked on planet Earth. If you had been able to meet one, however, it would not have harmed you – unless you threatened it. This was because it did not eat meat but lived only on plants.

Crane neck

Brachiosaurus had a very long neck. It could raise and lower its neck like a crane and swing it from side to side using the strong muscles in its chest. The bones in its neck were hollow. This made them light in weight. Muscles stretching from its back and up its neck helped **Brachiosaurus** hold its head up without much effort.

Powerful tail

Brachiosaurus's tail was long and powerful. The dinosaur probably held its tail up in a way that helped balance the weight of its neck. **Brachiosaurus** may have used its tail as a weapon in attacks by meat-eating dinosaurs.

Big nostrils

Just above this dinosaur's eyes, on top of its head, were two very large nostrils.

Scientists once thought it needed these to breathe in water. However, we now know it lived mostly on land. Instead, the nostrils may have been used to make snorting noises for communicating with other dinosaurs. They might also have been

foot. Most of the time, it walked on its toes.

Useful stones
Because it had no grinding teeth, **Brachiosaurus** had to gulp its food whole. It swallowed small, rough stones, too. The stones helped grind the food in its stomach. But they soon became worn smooth.

used to take in large amounts of air, which helped cool the animal down. These large nostrils probably gave **Brachiosaurus** a good sense of smell.

Big feet
At the ends of **Brachiosaurus's** straight, thick legs were broad, round feet. You can count the number of toes it had. The toe bones in its front feet were a little longer than those on the back feet and more like the bones in a hand than a

Brachiosaurus then spat them out and looked for more stones to swallow.

The Sauropod family

Brachiosaurus (1) belonged to a family, or group, of dinosaurs called **Sauropods**. They were all very large and had long necks, heavy bodies, and long tails. They lived in different parts of the world but were all herbivores, feeding on trees and plants growing along riverbanks.

Camarasaurus (KAM-AR-A-SAW-RUS) **(2)**, one of the smaller members of this family, lived in the area we now call North America about 145 million years ago. It looked very much like its cousins, but its neck and tail were shorter, and its back legs were longer than its front ones.

Camarasaurus means "chambered lizard." It gets this name from the hollow spaces scientists found in its long backbone.

Supersaurus (SUPER-<u>SAW</u>-RUS) **(3)** was even bigger than its cousin **Brachiosaurus**. Its name means "super lizard." **Supersaurus** may be renamed when scientists find more of its bones and know more about this huge dinosaur.

But another **Sauropod, Ultrasaurus** (<u>ULL</u>-TRA-<u>SAW</u>-RUS) **(4)**, may have been larger still than its cousin, **Supersaurus**. Its name means "gigantic lizard," and it was possibly the biggest **Sauropod** of all.

Some of its bones were first discovered in Colorado, in the United States, only a few years before you were born. Scientists are still studying them.

GLOSSARY

carnivores — meat-eating animals.

droppings — animal body wastes.

extinction — the dying out of all members of a plant or animal species.

graze — to feed on grass or other plants that grow in a field or pasture.

herbivores — animals that survive by eating plants.

herd — a group of animals that travels and lives together.

massive — very large and heavy.

mate — to join together (animals) to produce young.

predators — animals that kill other animals for food.

snout — protruding nose and jaws of an animal.

INDEX